A FILAMENT BURNS IN BLUE DEGREES

A FILAMENT BURNS
IN BLUE DEGREES

 *poems*
Kendra Tanacea

 LOST HORSE PRESS
Sandpoint, Idaho

ACKNOWLEDGMENTS

The author gratefully acknowledges the following publications in which these poems first appeared:

5 A.M.: "Closing Argument," "Rush," "Dusk," Childless," "Haiku," and "Speed"
Barely South Review: "Thanksgiving"
The Coachella Review: "In Flight"
Juked: "When It Happened"
Licking River Review: "Divorced at Forty"
Moon City Review: "Diagnosis"
San Diego City Works Press: "First Born, Still Born"
Pearl: "Daughter" and "Why You Should Never Marry a Psychiatrist"
Pebble Lake Review: "After the Funeral" and "A Filament Burns in Blue Degrees"
Rattle: "Stepmother"
Stickman Review: "Memorial"

I'm grateful to many who have helped me along the way. Among them are Ed Ochester, Amy Gerstler, Susan Kinsolving, Henri Cole, Kim Addonizio's Writing Workshops, Natalie Shapero, Leslie McGrath, the Bennington Ladies, Thea Sullivan's Intuitive Writing Workshops, Christopher P. DeLorenzo and the Laguana Writers.

And my partner in all things, John W. Diehl and, of course, my mother, Loretta Caranica Tanacea.

Cover Photograph: "Keepsake" © John W. Diehl. jwdiehl.homestead.com.
Author Photo: John W. Diehl.
Book & Cover Design: Christine Holbert.

FIRST EDITION

This and other Lost Horse Press titles may be viewed online at www.losthorsepress.org.

LIBRARY OF CONGRESS CATALOGING-IN-PUBLICATION DATA

ISBN 978-0-9968584-8-9

Library of Congress Cataloging-in-Publication Data is available from the Library of Congress.

CONTENTS

II.

III.

ONE

MISUNDERSTANDING

A purple aster grows
from my left nipple,
the leafy vine curving
upward. Deep blossom.

I'm topless, kissing my husband
in an alley. With a pair of scissors,
he clips the aster from its base, says,

you didn't weed before you came
to me. I'm silent, not knowing
how to explain: flower, not weed.

SPEED

With him, there was always ecstasy and Club
Universe. When that closed, the End Up.

And, after that, his basement apartment on Fulton.
Tin foil taped to window panes. No light there.

The last time I saw him, he stole twenty dollars
from my purse, then called from jail, *the irony*, he said,

when I pulled out my license, the crystal fell out.
After his family took him home to Minnesota, I found yellow

Post-its, the smallest ones, covered with his blue writing, stuck
all over the frame of his computer, continuing high up the wall.

Decision trees: (a) ask Julie to marry me; explain
kid-like-change-of-heart; (b) depending on how that goes,

tell the Romanian you miss having sex with her, explain
kid-like-heartbreak; (c) only three more months of *Playboy*

online subscription. Yellow tab after yellow tab.
When he finally called, he said there were germs everywhere,

pausing to spray the receiver with Lysol. Once, in bed,
he showed me a black and white shot of himself: a two-year-old

in front of the tinseled and sparkly Christmas tree with the barrel
of a realistic toy pistol in his mouth.

A FILAMENT BURNS IN BLUE DEGREES

This cold light.
Crumbs. Drops of jelly

on the cabinet. My hair
damp. Curled and tangled.

I want to half-know:
a refrigerator door, slightly open.

On a shady shelf. Things lifted
from me. Come to me like the sneak

of chocolate I am. Crack the ice,
swing the bins open into a light

with no promise. I'm your
fresh storage. And caloric.

Come after midnight, your hand
on the door, and me, lit, humming.

PHOTOSENSITIVE

In the shadow box at the Exploratorium,
just before our wedding, we held hands and jumped.
The flash shot off, our shadows froze
on the white panel behind us.

Our likeness only lasted for seconds, then faded
to white. We jumped again, loving our poses,
our silhouettes together, my ponytail high in the air.
We were faceless, but looked like family.

BOYS I PROMISED TO LOVE FOREVER

Greg, Tom, Kevin. How many trees
I graffitied with names and symbols,
interlocking initials. A tree on Tashua Road.
A tree on Barn Hill Road. A tree that still

grows within the boundaries of that yard.
How confident I was that I could love forever,
audaciously proclaiming it again and again.
Names, hearts recklessly carved into bark.

RUSH

Ice cubes clink in the tumbler.
A blade chops, elongates lines on a mirror.
The heart picks up.
The shy undressing.
Tightly rolling a dollar bill.
Breathing deep. Slow.
The horse stomping dust clouds at the starting gate.
Touching shoulder blades, clavicle, his straight nose.
The one with pure skin. Knowable bones.
Dopamine spilling forth.
Kissing closed eyelids, tracing the jawbone.
Rolling a joint, licking the seal.
Just two bodies, no blankets.
A thin veil of sweat.
The body producing its own opiates,
stunning me time after time.
Sprinters, fingers at the line.
Just before the shot rings out.

SABBATH

In the flat upstairs, the girls are getting it on.
Six am and the bang-banging
headboard. Creaks. *Ohs* and *ohs...*
I say, *go sisters!*
Now that's church:

preacher, choir, congregation.
The divine mystery of
how two people sound
together, the bed's legs scraping
hardwood floors. God bless

balloon framing, sound travel.
Let's get busy thin sheetrock.
A neighbor broomsticked his ceiling.
Sinner! Let all loud lovers
proclaim their faith.

Here comes my sleep-late lover,
taking the still warm cup
from my hands.
Yesses and *oh my gods.*
You bet I fell to my knees.

WITHOUT SOUND

Only in thick night could I mouth,
I love you, my voice, a hairline crack.

Shifting sheets, clearing my throat, I turned
my naked self over and over in this bed,

our library. When the door closed,
there was an eerie light that drafted

through door slats, haloed the edges
of drawn shades. Contained there, we

could never fully dam that glorious leakage.
What I've said remains between us. So breakable.

Wrap it in tissue paper, place it in a dark cupboard,
even separate the crystal bell from its clapper.

HOSTAGE

I'm yours completely, mouth silver
with duct tape, wrists rope-burned.
On tiptoe, I dangle

from the center beam, crystals
hanging from my nipples.
You pull the rope tighter.

My spine straightens, my hair
hangs braided. I can't imagine
what you're going to do.

Lipstick pink walls. Cracked plaster.
Headless dolls everywhere,
naked, armless mannequins.

In the mirror, my own eyes scare
me. You sit down, naked and hairless
in the dark corner, smoking.

The end burns. There's no point in struggling.
That's why I'm here. I'm carefree.

My white skin glows.

MAKING RISOTTO FOR DINNER
WHEN HIS EX-WIFE CALLS

While I mince an onion, he talks with her,
planning their son's bar mitzvah, sounding
so familiar, so nuts and bolts. Turning up the gas flame,
I sauté the onion translucent. Butter sizzles, foams,
as they go over the invitation list, names I've never heard.

Adding a cup of Arborio, I think of white rice
thrown high in the air by the fistful. I pour
two glasses of chardonnay, one for the risotto,
one for myself, sip, then gulp. Blend.

The band, flowers, menu?
Heady, I stare at the recipe to orient myself, to understand
what I am doing: *Add broth, cup by cup, until absorbed.*
Add Parmesan. Serve immediately.

The word *immediately* catches my eye,
but their conversation continues, then his son
gets on the line and hangs up on him,
as I stir and stir, holding the wooden spoon.

AUBADE

Before first light, the clouds are smoky.
So purple. The bedroom window perspires,
and, across the street, artificial light floods

the church's gold cross. Blackbirds fly off the eaves,
swoop, return. It's him, I think, through night,
through fog, his skin, his hairless chest.

In dreams, I reach around his waist, roam
under his shirt, my hands under this fabric,
this opaque memory.

The cars are quiet, parked and dark. The birds
take off again, swoop over the street, return.
Why didn't I touch him like this before?

Confident hands running from nipples to waistband,
down the spine. Books are splayed open on the bed,
hefty novels with complex plots. Rivulets

streak the window. Crumpled tissues bloom
from the bedspread, these white carnations
among the bright lupines, dahlias, delphiniums.

The doorknob, that diamond, throws firelight.
Gray-purple turns blue-blue and fills the room.
He's bare, lying there, his chest smooth,

but the paper thuds on the front steps and the birds
take off in a huge V, flapping overhead, veering,
then dissolving over power lines.

KEYHOLE

Down on both knees, one eye,
iris and pupil, looking
through the elliptical.
Just behind that locked door.
Shadows.
Dark corners, wood floor,
the braided rug, searched for clues.
A sheer black thigh, the silver glint
from a belt buckle.
A static quilt with its patchwork.
What is happening just out of sight?
Dresser drawers open, close.
Clothes are shed, drop to the floor.
Hinges and floorboards creak.
There is the scent of man, of woman, of cedar.
The eye shifts, straining in its socket.
French doors open onto a veranda
overlooking an ivy-walled garden.
The round moon is rising, giant and yellow.
Star jasmine, star jasmine!
An eye can see far beyond
its scope: solar systems, galaxies,
the Milky Way's skid of stars.
All atoms, revolving around one another.
Asteroids, shooting stars, comets.
Balls of ice with fire tails.
Red dusty planets. Resonant rings,
rotating and rotating,
that skeleton key. Unlock me.

CUP OF BLUE

This morning, steam
curls from the lip
of my blue mug, winds

its way up. The sun,
a white ball, low
and cold, behind

the black palm. I hold
this cup in both hands,
remembering you, eyes

closed as the sun rose,
your mouth against my ear.
Your words, forgotten.
But the heat.

There's no warmth
in this sun, the tea, the blanket.
The panes of glass are frosty

and my hair grows long
and wild as I wait
for you to appear.

The dog barks at the closed door.
But the knob doesn't turn, the stair
doesn't creak, no one calls out *hello*.

STATUESQUE

I've seen you in a museum before,
the aquiline nose, arrogant nostrils.
Addressing your stiff back, I ask
if you want something to eat.

You can't even see me
with those blank, Grecian eyes,
or turn your torso, so exquisitely
marbled with blue veins.

If I had a chisel, I would drive
it in on an angle, just over the place
your heart should be.

TILL DEATH DO US PART

Here's the rain. She opens
cellar doors, descends

into this damp place, trying
to save what she can.

Afraid of this dark, groping
for the hanging string

of one bare light bulb. Cobwebs

across her face. Framed and nailed
above her a yellowed front page:

Dewey Defeats Truman.
There's no certainty in facts.

Yet this cellar still floods.
She tries to raise things

to prevent further damage:
warping of wood, rusting

of steel, paper's disintegration.
An old Timex display case,

fluorescent and turning: rose quartz,
fool's gold, a vial of mercury.

She drops liquid silver
into her palm. Poisonous.

Beautiful flow, streaming
thinly forward,

never separating, then gathering
itself back into a reflective ball.

BRUISE

Have you ever seen a nine-iron
smack a fleshy thigh? Angry
skin turns red, then darkens
from holding its breath then hides
in the folds of a spring dress.

What doesn't turn black
is the deepest blue, the sky
just before dark.

Have you really seen the stars?
A closed fist against your temple,
the buzzing, the flares,
a spectacular rain of them.

THANKSGIVING

Carving a turkey, basted by his ex-wife,
around a table in this fall night. Children, dog at hearth.

Alone in your flat, loneliness settles in the chest:
phlegm. Dark meat sitting in watery gravy.

You're home, while the man you sleep with clears
his ex-wife's plate. I mean, she's there in his house,

the one you've been naked in, wandering the kitchen,
looking for a snack in the shadow of Mount Tam.

It's a cold place. Even his dog barks when you kiss,
and you are what you are: a stranger in a family's home.

You walked yourself stupid today, to the ocean and back,
hoping to lose yourself in the people carrying yams

and pecan pies from their cars to front doors. You want
to stop imagining the scene, the setting and clearing,

the dumb domesticity of it all, scraps to the dog,
playing Pictionary, renting a movie. You think,

this is what I was meant to be: a sorry animal
aggravating her own wound. This persistent cough:

jealousy. Every ugly thing gathered into a cornucopia
of grievances: Thanksgiving.

ELECTRICAL STORM

The picture tube blue-sparks,
then shatters. After that, no images,
just sound. Turning toward the dark
window, she thinks she hears

a thousand crows tapping the glass,
trying to get her attention. *Calm down*,
he says, *it's just the computer*.
The grinding of data on the hard drive.

She doesn't know when he last logged on.
No blueprints for his chat rooms;
he's learned how to erase the history.
On the screen, there's just a confusion

of galactic stars rushing at her.
Best not to look. Instead, she sips
white wine from the glass he hands her,
the rim thin and fragile at her lip.

The sofa doesn't give when his thigh
accidentally touches hers. Sound keeps coming
from the dead screen, dialog from *Six Feet Under*.
Affairs, open relationships. Everyone is cheating.

Please don't leave me. I have to end it.
We never had sex. Don't tell her.
He won't even side-glance in her direction.
In her mind, she's watching

Wait Until Dark: a blind woman smashing
every light bulb in her basement apartment
to even the playing field. She douses that con-
man with gasoline, then lights a match.

WHY YOU SHOULD NEVER MARRY
A PSYCHIATRIST

He'll tell you that his ex-wife is a *borderline*, his last girlfriend was *labile* and *dysphoric*, his son has *issues*, so you'll begin to wonder where you fit in, diagnostically. He'll ask you to express your needs, then point out that you're projecting all over him, calmly explaining that you are seeing him as your bad father: *You need therapy.* He'll say that your reaction to him turning inward (or ignoring you) is catastrophic. Your therapist will explain that your husband is a *narcissist*, but you'll counter that he runs around all day attending to the needs of others in a save-the-world manner. Your therapist will then explain that he is a *covert narcissist*, invested in his role as do-gooder. Imagine bugged rooms, hidden cameras, conspiracies! Everyone in your new family will be medicated: Adderall for your husband's ADD and as a hedge against depression, Zoloft for his son's anxiety. Soon you'll ask your therapist for Valium just to get through the day. You'll become thin and tired, and your husband will suggest B-12 shots, and you'll begin to question what is really happening, if all your energy and interpretive power has been zapped as part of this covert operation. Near the end, he'll fuck you just before Shabbas dinner, come, then run right into the shower. When you complain, he will blankly ask if you feel exploited. He'll accuse you of not being *present*, tell you that sometimes you withdraw so far you are inscrutable. And that's the moment you finally feel free, then you begin to wonder: what am I doing here? He'll tell you he can't give you rhapsodic love—when really, it's the only thing you want, if you were to express yourself—and that he can't handle you with kid gloves. And you'll think to yourself, if you won't, who will? And you'll realize that this man you vowed to love until death do you part is an *asshole, a covert narcissist with a martyr complex*, and you will leave him at a restaurant just as he lifts a piece of sushi with his chopsticks.

STEPMOTHER

Because he hates chocolate, you'll bake lemon cakes
and lemon tarts, trying to make the sour sweet.

You'll ride roller coasters with him until you are dizzy
and sick and the whole world is spinning.

Your husband will ask you to leave, and you will, taking long walks
alone in the shade of the redwoods, or wandering the aisles

of Safeway until you are asked to return. In the morning,
when you are naked in bed, covered only by a thin sheet,

this boy will walk in. You'll stiffen like a corpse,
remembering that Tom told you when he was thirteen

all he wanted to do was look at his stepmother's breasts.
Your husband will chide you for failing to pour him a cup

of cranberry juice or neglecting to toast a bagel, convincing
evidence you have no maternal instincts. He will finger

through all your things and you'll start sleeping with
your clothes on and your purse at your side.

You'll police yourself so carefully that you are no longer yourself,
just a ghost of a woman who silently slips in and out of bed.

And you'll realize the trouble you're in when the young boy
at Albertsons carries your groceries all the way to your car,

smiles, says, *good to see you*, asks how you're doing.

ARCHITECTURE OF MEMORY

hello lover
step back into our old home
overhead beams so low
align past & present
in the camera's aperture

our way of making love
familiar as Coppertone
erase & rub up memory
ultraviolet light on ferro-gallate
an insoluble blueprint

beneath our room's wallpaper
a border of high-gloss daisies
enamel over latex peach
before that studs & sheetrock
before that an open patio

tonight your skin's carbon paper
the way you handle me
reams of smudged copies
kissing & kissing &
cannon-balling off the high-dive

remember the torn-down I-Beam
now condos & ATMs
but before that Sunday tea dances
layers of stapled poster art &
the always-spinning disco ball

our granular silhouettes
an architectural palimpsest
what we built over ruins
dayglo strobe-shadows
in the black light of our lost city

AFFAIR

Afterwards, S. says, *this will always stay in my memory.*
How neat! Like a rolled-up ball of socks in a dark drawer.
I suppose he meant it in an elegiac way, but still, I couldn't
quite understand. Didn't nature design memory to fail
to survive the accumulation of grief?

Even the memory of my first husband, the one, I thought,
the body, I thought, I would never forget
like the curves on the drive home, I'm forgetting.
All that's left of my grandfather: a few instamatic photos,
now faded eerie green. I can't remember more except

that his wife's mind glitched at sixty-two from a stroke.
Just one biological mishap can erase a lifetime
of memories. Needle on a scratched record,
for years she only said, *Oh mother, oh mother . . .*
Other than that, she was speechless.

How will one night in a plain hotel room maintain prominence
when my long film-reel years have already been misplaced?
Maybe S. has lasting memories of a sweeter kind,
how his mother applied pink lipstick before church,
then blotted her lips on delicate tissue.

Me, I work hard at forgetting the way a pan of boiling hot dogs
flew across our kitchen. How mirrors were broken. Golf clubs
used as weapons. That moment I held a cast iron pan
with both hands ready to bring it down.
Forget. Forget. Forget.

TWO

WHEN IT HAPPENED

When Dad came home from the hospital, Donna Summer
on the radio. A blue robe. Welcome home! Detoxing,

there were ghosts: his mother white-nightgowning toward him
through the center of his bed. Back of his neck, railroad-stitched,

just over the cervical spine. Christmastime? The Super-8's
flood light so bright he's squinting. *Hold up the new robe!*

Blondie was singing about hearts of glass and either there were icicles
or it was hot and humid. A tropical dress on a heavy July night.

Sometimes I think it was January, his car skidding on black ice.
Other times I'm sure it's July and summer vacation, tuning the radio

to catch a song and a breeze through the screen. Set the table,
wash the dishes, just one long Formica day.

He was there, then he was gone. He came back.
It was Christmas and we gave him a blue robe. To lounge,

to recover. Recover. But it was July in the heat of summer
when I was a nurse in *South Pacific*. That's when he got sick.

Or became sick. When he spent long nights in the basement,
magnifying quartz, pyrite, slices of mica. The cellar:

the coolest place on those sleepless nights, radio crackling,
the antenna unable to grab onto a station.

A STRANGE EXPLOSION IN SCORPIO

In my father's brain, double stars
are merging. He says, *I've been sober*

38 pounds. Convinced he's dying
of cancer, he's offloading all his wealth:

quartz with a water bubble
trapped inside, gold tiger's eye.

Take the Tiger Woods!
Take the Tiger Woods!

In my fist, my inheritance.
Kissing me, he says: *You're a good man.*

What looks like a scorpion can also be
a leaning coconut tree, a brooded swan.

When two stars orbit each other so closely,
their outer layers touch, then flare:

a solitary red nova.

INSTRUCTIONS FROM THE SUN

In winter's slant-light, follow me.
    It's still warm where I am.

Cross the street, take my arm.
    I know it seems our time together

may be over, but remember the eclipse?
    We stood, facing each other,

on that narrow path of totality, a new moon
    between us. Even then, my corona

streamed. And my returning flash, a perfect diamond.
    But who knows how long we can

withstand the forces of this love?
    Some say it's my death, but even then,

stay with me, an exploding supernova.
    So bright, momentarily outshining

the galaxy. Then, no light, just the pull
    of gravity. Still recognize me?

Spiral in, my companion star.

PRACTICALLY SPEAKING

Tonight, the moon is full. Forget
about the moon, the water heater
must be replaced. Hot water

is everywhere, overflowing
the steel tank, warping wood,
dissolving plaster. I said

forget about the moon.
It's just a flimsy
science fair exhibit:

just drill a clean hole through
a speckled granite slab, balance
on faux columns. Jury-rig

a bare light bulb above, using cheap
knob and tube wiring. This system
can short at any time

and the pink pillars
supporting this heavy night
are already showing stress cracks.

SEPARATION

I keep returning to a candlelit
house. A drawn, blue
bathtub. Pouring champagne,
my hand shakes: a tremor.
Blue flutes, cut glass, red
lipstick, a black slip.

Before I destroyed our home
with engineered stone and
veneer, there were built-ins
and heat from the oven.
From crowbar to cracking plaster,
dust floured my hair. Then, I was
old. Eyelids folded over.

When I was young, I made
shoebox homes, dioramas
of families, walls slick with blue
vinyl butterflies. Where's the lagoon,
the upside-down kayak? Sunlight
bending rows of delphiniums?

Tonight, a strong gust strums the guitar,
as dead leaves fly around the solitary
purple sofa. The house steams
from boiling spaghetti and I step out
of my clothes as if I were calmly
walking out of a burning building,
a trail of lava blackening behind me.

SPEECHLESS

I could have done without the scene
of my key coming off your ring.
I had my hands on that weak
orange vase, but thought better

of throwing it. *Why say anything?*
I said only to myself.
There's no understanding a bicep
when its tendons are paralyzed.

You have muscles, I used to say,
counting out ten perfect push-ups.
Oh thoughtless barbells, sitting
dumbly in the corner. But you cheated:

pushing up one bicep with your other hand.
I was talking, saying, explaining,
saying nothing, really, not making my point,
words raining down like passionless

lightning. I used to think words were
florescent finials: obvious, interesting,
useful.

So, I've lost my faith,

watching dreary sushi float by
in a miniature boat.
Did I say I used to believe in words?
Please just hold me, whirl me around

this depressed parquet floor. Just lead.
A gentle hand, a subtle shift
in your weight. I'm turning
in my dictionary and all sentences

for this new way of speaking:
fox-trot me.

DIVORCED AT FORTY

A woman unloads her dishwasher,
bone china clanking against itself
as a strange man pulls off her roof

tiles. He sends the debris down
a chute off her kitchen where a blue
landing with a spiral staircase

circles down into the ivy-walled
garden where a green tent holds
the remains of a banquet: abandoned

white plates, cake crumbs, flat champagne
in flutes near the gazebo made of sea shells,
translucent and beaded with dew in pink

hollows that she gently brushes
the moisture from.
                    At dusk the man

leaves on the landing a small shed,
the perfect playhouse for some child,
a lean-to frame, the pane windows

facing the setting sun. She crowbars
it apart, sending splintered wood
down the chute to the alley below.

TO MY STEPSON

That June day, you, bare-chested,
massaged by two girls in bikinis at the park.
That night, I laid a washcloth soaked in vinegar

and water over your back to cool the burn.
You started to cry. Why?
Serious boy, your calves were your father's,

your fingers moved so quickly, so lightly
over the guitar's bronze strings. We two-stepped
together, you showed me your moves on the deck,

we lit sparklers and exploded
orange smoke bombs against that night,
the night your father proposed. Remember

dancing the hora at your bar mitzvah? Remember
eating moon cakes in Chinatown? Remember feeding
the nene in Kauai? Those birds ate out of our hands.

EVERYTHING BREAKS IN A MOVE

Cracked dishes, the ones I love,
gone. Espresso cup, porcelain teapot.

Remember the stars, how they used to be?
Visible, close and bright.

Maybe a skylight.
Through the window's bars, broken mirrors.

I look so strange cut up at the kitchen sink.
Out of bubble wrap, forgotten landscapes appear:

a redhead seated on the world holding
a martini glass, Jupiter rising over her ear;

a lost girl carrying a suitcase, blue earth
and gold sky showing right through her.

PERSPECTIVE

Why did we start at the *Bitter End*
with a plate of greasy fish and chips?
There, we shared a couple of seven-and-sevens,
even said a few things, but my poor
circulation and cold hands affected him,
although he swears by a high metabolism.

He was too tall and that scares me: the difference
in perspective. God, he felt warm. I swear
I wasn't thinking of Michael, but his mind
was on Lisa, that place where he left
his bed frame, his mattress, where another
man now sleeps. But still, he said, I looked

like Venus, rising from an iridescent shell,
from the calm sea, hair swirling.
There was a numb frost I brought
to the evening, thinking: this is not magic.
Now, I'm a born-again realist, so he was a nice,
tall man who had a good and constant

body temperature. I daringly touched his shoulder
blades: Careful! Don't cut yourself! Compelled
to expose all myths (Santa, the Tooth Fairy, etc.),
I deflated all that was rising. Lying there, not talking,
felt good if, for nothing else because, for an instant,
we were hoping for something outside of ourselves.

I didn't tell him he was the first man I'd kissed
since the divorce because I was too busy looking
for the disappearing quarter and the missing rabbit.

He crumpled under my coolness, became a light,
hollow man who owned an iron and an ironing board
and a round, white rug I circumnavigated on my way out.

PHANTOM PAIN

Even when you know your leg is missing,
stabbing pains. They say
it's biological, not psychological.
Nerve paths never change, so the brain
can never accept the foot is gone.

In my dreams, I script alternate endings.
Sometimes I hug him under the evergreens,
then walk alone down the dirt path.
Last night, he sat beside me at a movie.

Under our skin are many receptors for pain,
the intensity just as vivid years later.
A beard, a belly.
Even though I know he's gone, inside
a new woman, he's still inside me.

They say every character in a dream
is just a side of the dreamer. So the man
in the theater is me. Sometimes I embrace
his new wife, kiss them both on the cheek.

But they are all me.
I'm loving me. Kissing me.

IN FLIGHT

A dense cloud cover.
No horizon and a faulty altimeter.

No orientating moon.
Have you flown like this before?

Hoping the disconnected self can return
from a flatline. Apply the defibrillator,

and the soul high in the corner
will merge back into its body.

A runway lined with white lights
and the magnetic pull of earth.

Like those who stepped out of the fuselage,
wandering lost in an endless cornfield.

They never thought they were in Iowa.
They thought: this is heaven.

NEW HOME

Stripped to the studs, the hollow echoes.
I used to blueprint a nursery, our bedroom.

Now, I move walls, cut openings, expand.
It's gutted, but the joists are solid.

New sheetrock, fresh white paint,
hard wiring for greater amperage.

Easy to fall in love with the graying carpenter,
the plumber who tells me exactly how to fix

these corroded pipes. These men are here
to help. We have taken the old refrigerator

to the dump, with its carton of soured
milk still inside.

MILEAGE

I worry now when my father
drives the dog to the park.
The car's too old.
There they go.
There they all go.
The brakes are bad.
There's a toothpick wedged in the console
to stop the hazards from blinking.
The odometer just rolled over 250,000
so we're all holding our breath.
The car cools in the dark garage.
My father naps during the day,
TV too loud, heat too high.
The dog doesn't jump on the bed
anymore or turn graceful circles.
Just slumps, bones hitting ground.
The car takes awhile to start.
They hesitate to take long trips.
The oil leaks but my father keeps filling it up.
The dog's nose bleeds.
Today, my father grabbed the handrail.
The dog has trouble breathing at night.
A cancerous polyp.
My father can't sleep at night,
so he massages the dog's paws.
He loves this, he says.
The old dog looks like he does.
They are moving in slow motion,
the way my father leaves the house,
the way the dog rises and follows him,
the tired car door opening,
accepting them both. The dog sighs,
turns to look back,
his white mask in the rear window.

FATHER

He reached for the ivory scrimshaw bottle with its etched-blue sailboat.
Slapped aftershave on each cheek, saying, *You're a good looking son-of-a-gun,*

don't ever die, clicking two imaginary pistols at the mirror. I dabbed
it behind my ears. *You smell like the perfume counter at Woolworths,*

he said. I knew how to handle the gold razor too: twist the bottom,
the trap doors open. Lathering up a cake of soap with the shaving brush,

we swirled cream over cheeks, upper lip, neck. With our thumbs, we'd
clear a path over lips, then stick tongue in cheek for the closest shave.

THE PAST: A WORKING HYPOTHESIS

Although I decided not to go back, I've tried to get to
the bottom of things. Like most kids, I dug for China,
thinking I could pass through dirt, rock, lava, then emerge
through the crust of the earth. But I hit stone.

Getting to the bottom of things assumes a bottom.
Just as getting to the heart of things assumes its fixed position.
Eat all the leaves of an artichoke. Where are you then?

I decided not to go back because the new psychology says
it's the relating between patient and therapist that cures,
not the simple retrieval of the past. So I'm not going back.
Not to the past.

And I'm not getting to the bottom of things either.
I've discarded my shovel, my trowel.
I'm not even sure where the heart is located anymore.

I've decided not to go back to anatomy books,
to dissected frogs, to places where my heart expanded
and the places where it staggered. I refuse to perform proofs,
analyze syllogisms, or figure out how to park my VW van

next to the Camaro but nowhere near the Cadillac. I won't
weigh things in grams or moles or figure out speed, distance,
density or mass. Mrs. Conley taught us Zeno's dichotomy paradox:
that a person could never mathematically walk through a door.

Because distance is always divided in half, you get closer
and closer to the threshold, but ultimately, never reach it.
(I didn't believe it then and don't believe it now.)
And not going back means circling overhead,

some may say like a bird, but I say like a Blue Angel.
There are high-speed loops and sophisticated stunts.
And no purpose or mission whatsoever.
Just white circles temporarily scraped in the air.

CLOSING ARGUMENT

You heard the expert on narcissism and have the DSM-5 diagnostic criteria for your reference. Remember he taught me to play *Helpless* on guitar? Maybe it was all transference. Tonight was my father's seventy-second birthday. I kept the yellow Post-It he stuck on my knee: *You're such a wonderful daughter*. Exhibit A.

In his last email, which has been entered into evidence as Exhibit B, he wrote: *Normal, expectable human emotions are a mere indulgence*. And he's a psychiatrist! It was impossible to prove to him that I loved him—and I'm a lawyer. So he proved what he was trying to disprove: that I would leave. It seems like fraud or negligent misrepresentation. I think we've both made that case.

On Valentine's Day, I wrote him two poems he didn't read. I had stapled them to the biggest card I could find at Walgreens because my love was cheap, trite and sentimental. Fool. In verse, I described his sculpted buttocks, how his balls felt like ripe figs, that our love was religious.

So, ladies and gentlemen, I said it all, but he couldn't hear me because he's fifty and beginning to lose his hearing. And he couldn't see me because he wore those drugstore glasses all the time. He kept stringing and re-stringing guitars, buying and selling them on Ebay. Sometimes he would play in bed while I sucked him, singing *When Will I Be Loved?*

MEMORIAL

for my Grandfather

Every Sunday, church. In his gold shirt.
On Easter, in his black overcoat and buttonholed
carnation, he carved lamb from a spit in our yard.
Later, we danced in a tight circle. Opa! *Papu*.

When his daughter was born, he paid for the delivery
with an inlaid chest, fitting all those pieces together:
the concerned doctor, chin in hand, the feverish child,
the lantern's honey-stained light.

On April Fools' Day, his wife's birthday, he carved
the skin off an orange in a continuous spiral,
recomposed it into a perfect whole, placed it
in the wooden fruit bowl.

When she could no longer speak, he made her
an easy chair. And combed her gray hair
and built us a home with its bones
on the outside. All those years of scaffolding.

After thirty years of piecework, after arthritis
bowed his fingers, he carved a chair for the bishop
with a relief of St. George, riding a rearing horse,
spearing the open-mouthed dragon.

He carved at night. Steady hand, chisel,
curlicues of wood. Sawdust resting in the wrinkles
of his pants, on his white mustache, in the hollow
of his good ear.

When he became ill, he sank into the loveseat
by the plate-glass window. In silhouette,
his Einstein hair, Philip of Macedon nose,
and slight paunch that grew with cancer.

That February before he died, he carved Lincoln
out of snow. Great man seated on his chair,
chiseled features. At dusk, he splashed it
with water and, overnight, it iced like marble.

RIDER

Monroe, Connecticut

Riding bareback
across Pulaski's farm,
the mare's long hair
in my fists.

After my fall,
after the concussion,
I learned how to hold on.

Sorèze, France

Corralled together, two horses kissing.
Really kissing with their tongues.
My first impulse was to turn away.
But I couldn't.

The chestnut Stallion circled
the Appaloosa, pounding out
dust clouds with his hooves.
The sky was indigo.

They had no riders, no obligations.
They bit each other affectionately.

Pescadero, California

My stepson extended
his arm over the fence,
offering a snapped carrot
to the black Arabian.

I permitted this, worrying
about his wild nature.
        But he took it

gently, then pressed his muzzle
against my neck, into that small
spot reserved for lovers.

Morelia, Mexico

My husband and I rode uphill,
on Spanish Mustangs into
the dusty woods.

Monarchs moved in all directions,
perching on our heads, my chest.

The sky was endlessly beating.
Orange and black. The heat.
We could hardly breathe.

Monroe, Connecticut

So young, Gail could easily lift me
onto the bony-backed Palomino.
Hold on to the mane.
She slapped its ass.

Feeding time. The horse turned
on a dime.
Whoa—
But instinct overrides command.

The speed, incredible, but brief.
Tall, dry grass blurring by.
I was slowly sliding off,
a coarseness slipping
between my fingers.

The split-second before
everything went black.

THREE

FIRST BORN, STILLBORN

It's hard to push out the dead.
I saw her once before, a fish
moving in liquid silver, a glassy-eyed
amphibian, somersaulting.

Her shoulders fold, like a nestled bird, against
my pubic bone. All I can think are the innards pulled
from roasting chickens, my hand twisting
in the cold, bony cavity, covered in watery blood.

The doctor tells me: *name her, cradle her,*
bury her, but I'd rather have the ether mask
from my tonsillectomy, counting backwards
into a black hole with pinpricks of purple light.

As I hold her, I remember my first doll.
During a fight over who would hold her,
my brother yanked off the arm.
We both stared at the glistening ball
and the torso's empty socket.

AFTER THE FUNERAL

We fill the dining room with lemon squares,
rolled dates, braided cookies, all dusted

with confectionary sugar, mounded on bone
china. A tray of apricot brandy is passed

and everyone, even the children, takes a swig,
spirits for the unbearable. Sweet bread, holy bread,

we offer our condolences twisted and baked into challah.
We fill hollowed watermelon shells with balls of honeydew

and cantaloupe, with a touch of lemon so they don't turn.
We compose plates for those who suffer: Here's a hot cross

bun or roast beef on a plain roll. The food keeps coming
through the door, each friend, each loved one, holding their grief

in a paper bag with handles, on a tray covered
with Saran wrap. No one eats their own dish,

knowing this sorrow. They sample a piece, a sliver,
of what all the others have brought, have laid on the table.

ORCHIDS

You left them all budding but stooped.
Orchids were beyond us, their need
for diffused light, measured sips of water.

Not confident in our abilities, we tied
their stems to pillars: Stand. Stand.

This evening, the moon's liquid light
fills the spare room. Down the hall,
the machine clicks. Your voice, distant

and thin, winds up the last odds and ends:
bills, your new number.

Tonight, I cut the twine, transplant
them at the foot of the bed.
My confederates, they stand guard.

Here's your light, your water.
Their spines straighten. Tender

casings open: bright, wide-eyed.

DAUGHTER

I want to be a woman who gets up early,
goes to the market with her daughter, feeling
each tomato, each avocado, making sure they are ripe.

At night, I want to be this woman chopping carrots,
slicing mushrooms. A green and white checkered apron
tied around my waist, my daughter setting the table,
filling the house with the chime of silverware.

We'd peel onions side by side, talking about all the tricks
that stop tears. But we'd cry anyway, our hips touching,
the wooden spoon stirred by her hand, then mine.

There is a soft whish as she peels. Vegetables snap
under my knife. Taste this, try that. We'd offer each other tips
of carrots, a scroll of bell pepper.

Everything in this kitchen is sweet and fresh. We'd pull apart
bread with our hands. The butter is soft and spreads easily.

NEGATIVE SPACE

A dome is an upside-down bowl
of emptiness. Every tube, a hollow
where nothing exists. But cast that place
in wet cement, pumped into Bramante's Tempietto,
pressed against the ceiling, the windows,
if the chapel was dismantled,
the exterior peeled off,
a concrete replica of interior space would exist;

it's the space between us when our hip bones meet;
the white vase between our profiles.
See what an empty bowl holds?
A flute has circumference, length, holes;
shoes have space for heels, arches, toes,
a ring, an open O;
and when our lips touch,
a crystal hourglass.

WHAT WOMEN OVER FORTY
WHO WANT CHILDREN DO

We get our blood drawn, compare
FSH numbers

like sport scores. We kick back
shots of Robitussin. We overdose

on vitamins. For the first time, we do it
missionary style, pillows under our hips,

leave the lights on all night. We do yoga,
acupuncture. We don't drink, but long to.

We keep ovulation calendars. We take
our temperature, chart and graph degrees

onto days, analyze the data like CEOs.
We pee on sticks, pray that God gives us

two blue lines. We are coaches,
cheerleaders: Go for it!

Touchdown! Score!

CREATION

The turkey baster is so old-fashioned. Now there's ICSI:
the doctor shoots an egg with a single sperm: POW!

In the dish, mitosis. Some divide too fast. Some too slow.
Only four out of seventeen are worth implanting.

Odds are only two will take; if not, selective removal
of the third is recommended. She only wants to implant

girl embryos. When he disagrees, she says,
you want a say, then you pay. If these eggs fail, scan

the websites of donors, girls selling young, fresh eggs
for twenty-thousand. Medical histories, eye color, height,

SAT scores and baby pictures. Forget romantic notions,
a strange woman's egg will join with your husband's sperm.

There's blood, but whose? Who will lay claim to motherhood?
There are contracts, typed and signed, but nothing has been proven

to hold up in court. Read the blogs. Couples mortgage their homes
for one more round. Better odds at Vegas. There are blood clots

and premies in incubators under a blue light. Acid reflux
and hearts too small to beat on their own. Tri-level strollers

and marriages collapsing under the weight. An embryo
waits on ice, ready to be thawed and inserted into a womb.

A two-pounder breathes through tubes,
breast milk injected straight into his belly button.

DIAGNOSIS

The sky is a gray x-ray. Here's the round moon
with cancer shadows. What looks like a church spire

is the spine with bone spurs and bulging discs.
It seems like an ordinary night,

I look like a woman with healthy hair, in a brown coat
that looks warm. Even as branches grab at the sky,

plum blossoms snow down like asbestos.
Sometimes the moon is a bullet hole,

sometimes the ultra-bright light from an otoscope.
The more the bones fail, the more I become this cool

exhale of menthol that hangs in the air. Everything sinks
so fast, like this moon over Telegraph Hill. I remember

a love so distracting that I slammed the car door on my own leg.
But that was only skin. My right hip keeps catching,

then giving out. Tension, inflammation? Or maybe
I'm carrying things too heavy for my frame.

Lesions and uncertainty. Radiation may help,
the way the Condor Club's red neon penetrates this fog.

HAIKU

A black branch. A wet petal. Silence. Nothing happening. It's as if she doesn't have to pay the rent or go to Trader Joe's or worry about that swerving car. I'd love to write three lovely lines about a frog, a pond, a ripple. The soft, silent snow. Sure, a flower might open, then close if you had all day to watch it. But life is more like jumping the turnstile, slipping through the subway doors. As for the rest, you just have to make it up as you go along. What about action? Things happen, right? I mean, that boy riding his bike just ran over a daisy, decapitated it. Quiet, peaceful moments don't exist on a MUNI line with the N Judah clanking by. Skateboarders. Car alarms. Shouting drunks. Anyway, things happen and should happen. Verbs, lots of them. Scram. Race. Burn rubber. Screech. The smell of burning clutch. Someone pounding on the wall to stop the bed from squeaking. If you have time to watch that morning glory open, I don't want to know you. It takes a lot to hold someone's attention these days with all those clever cuts and sound bites. I don't know about you, but *chop, chop*. Things have to get done. Check the oil, vacuum the rug, jackhammer the sidewalk. Even the tires need rotating. Do you stare out the window chewing on your eraser, thinking, *petal, ripple*? Or are you the one at midnight throwing rocks, trying to break the window of an abandoned warehouse?

PICTURE WINDOW

If you press your cheek against the pane,
and look down: magenta rhododendrons,
a stone wall.

At eye level, there's a narrow birdhouse
where generations of robins have lived,
learning, after a few fatalities, not to fly

into the living room. Squirrels roll
hickory nuts over the embankment.
Occasionally, a black lab passes.

It's a fixed square of crushed scenery,
trees and birds and flowers under
glass designed not to open.

I place both hands on it,
pressing my full weight.
The mitered frame holds us.

There are New Years and birthdays and ordinary
Sundays on one side. The woods, the sky,
a diminishing road on the other.

Some windows open. Some do not.
All I can do is leave fingerprints
and my breath on this cold glass.

ALONE IN KETCHIKAN

Here, it's spawning time. The river is swollen.
Salmon eggs, bright pennies in the riverbed.

Strange wakes appear on the river's surface,
pulses of water moving against the current.

In the estuary, sockeyes leap, twist and fling
themselves into the stream of their birth.

The tide slackens, current quickens. They surge
forward with singleness of purpose. It's misty, cold,

and my ovaries ache from the harvest: a steel needle
through the vagina. Freezing eggs,

everything on ice. These fish know better.
Refusing to eat, they turn red, fins and tails frayed

from beating the rocks, males fighting just to quiver
against a female, release their milt over those eggs.

Look up. Look up! Over there, a brown bear. Jaw
awe-wide, blinking, wading amid all this bounty.

CHILDLESS

I've almost forgotten about it, except
when the doctor says to put a bag of frozen peas

over my aching groin, my inflamed hip flexor,
and I think of genetic disasters, chemical

imbalances in the brain to comfort myself,
try to forget the name of my mythical daughter,

the one that never grew inside me, the one
that looks just like that embalmed fetus still

inside a dissected pregnant woman.
She knew she wasn't going to make it,

donated her body to be fully preserved,
her belly thinly sliced, exposing

the baby's spine pressed up
against her spine.

On a white block, she reclines suggestively,
hand on hip, mammary glands thrust forward,

the child entombed inside her.
Skinless, her secret is open

to all those who wanted to see
what they would rather forget.

THE LESSON

Tonight I'm the Niña, sailing the
round world, believing in flatness.

Imagine returning to where I began,
still fearing the dropping off.

What lack of progress. What relief.

DUSK

The Chinese elm outside my window
bleeds into the blue-twilight,
just before the blackness.
Blue pills pushed through foil:
the holes, harvest moons.
There's a steel sadness I carry.
How can I say it? So late . . .
How do people collect a family?
Here, I can draw my arms around myself
with certainty, familiarity.
The sky is dark now.
A steady drizzle.
Sometimes all I want is this loneliness.
To know there's no one
in this room to love.
The mind in isolation, rests.
Sadness frees me from worry.
There are things I can't hang on to:
affection, bodies.
I refuse to memorize his contours.
Ready for him to lift and evaporate.
The leaves are weighted and wet.
Outside, the tree lowers its canopy.
I wish I could say this is unfamiliar to me:
my hand on my crotch,
a solitary tree outside my window.

UNEARTHING

Three families will come, then
go next door.

The first will circle the magnolia
tree with a gravel path.

The second will saw it down, rip
out the stump and its ganglion, plant
banana trees, symmetrically,
on either side of the yard.

One won't make it, planted
in perpetual shade.
When it dies,

they'll ask me to cut down
my hawthorne trees. More sun.

Every year my trees leaf out in March.
In July, thirty bright green parrots
nest there, eating red berries.

The third family will remove
the dead tree, roll out sod.
You see, the wife is pregnant,
the flat too small.

BUILDING A TOWN

As every child with colored blocks knows,
all you need to build a town is a school,
a hospital, a church.

Oh, and of course, a house. Houses. Homes.
Curved streets and homes with blue shutters.
And flowers, windows with flower boxes.

And did I say people? Yes, people.

A silver-haired woman in a navy dress by the fountain.
One young boy sucking a lollipop in front of the church.
Two women in red jackets, arms linked, walking
toward the hospital.

And horses. A soft brown horse led by a man
in a gray cap. Two white horses in a pasture,
kissing.

Oh, and trees. Trees to line the curved streets.
And the church should have a bell that rings
every hour.

An owl and a rooster. And a black dog
with one blue eye and one eye brown. Park benches.
Lampposts. Geraniums. More trees. Families.

THUNDERSTORM

The night before I died, the sky
dropped its hard tears on my roof tiles.

The storm's insistence woke me.
Early in the morning, before the sun rose,

I walked along the dirt path, past round
hay bales and a church with no windows.

From this trail, I can't see the bell tower
or the fields of sunflowers. After the rain,

everything rises: rocks are bared, seeds
visible. Snails stretch their necks,

are bold enough to cross
my path. The grass is vibrating,

birds feast on naked worms. Everything
just under the surface, now exposed.

PERENNIAL

The rhododendron in Monroe
  from the picture window of my childhood home,

that gave us, every year, its first bloom on the fourth
  of June. Lilacs every April,

a constant hedge of baby's breath. These things
  still happen in my absence.

And, at the edge of the yard, where all my efforts cease,
  the wild tiger lilies are opening,

tangled in the forsythia,
  just where the woods begin.